SET
& DESCRIPTION
CHOOSING AND EVOKING PLACE

Amy Jones

Dedicated to Lilstock Beach, my childhood setting.
With thanks to editor Stephen Parsons.

Recommended further reading:
The Shakespearean Forest, Anne Barton, 2017
Setting, Jack M Bickham, 1999
The Art of Fiction, David Lodge, 1992
The Reith Lectures, Hilary Mantel, 2017
Description and Setting, Ron Rozelle, 2005
On Fairy Stories, J.R R Tolkien, 1939

Introduction	1
Set Why?	
Setting the Scene	2
Setting & Theme	4
Character & Place	6
Atmosphere & Mood	8
Set How?	
Description	10
Quality of Detail	12
Vision	14
Sound	16
Smell & Taste	18
Touch & Feeling	20
Recognisable Settings	22
Constrasting Settings	24
Set When?	
Past Settings	26
Present Settings	28
Future Settings	30
Multi-temporal	32
The Seasons	34
The Weather	36
Set Where?	
Sublime Earth	38
Above & Below	40
Settlements	42
Houses & Rooms	44
Institutions	46
Liminal Places	48
On the Road	50
Altered Settings	52
Fantasy Settings	54
Exercises	56

Detail from an old map of Lancaster, New York state, 1892

Introduction

Setting is perhaps the most overlooked aspect of the craft of writing. However, as this book will show, it is essentially impossible to tell any semblance of a story without some definable setting in time or place. The aim here is to help writers make even the most fantastic and abstract of settings 'true' for themselves and their readers without killing off their imagination or losing sight of the plot in an excess of detail.

Author and critic Carmen Maria Machado writes that *places are never just places in a piece of writing*. So how do settings shape the stories told within them? What do they reveal about the characters who inhabit them? And how do they reflect or subvert the real-world environments from which they draw inspiration? This book is designed to help authors explore the ways in which settings can establish mood and tone, develop characterization, propel narrative and make your writing more immersive.

We will consider 'macro' concepts about setting in place and time, examine a range of popular settings in fiction, and explore 'micro' details in describing aspects of setting through sensory and physical description. On the final pages, there are exercises based on discussions throughout the book to help writers struggling with setting to experiment with fresh perspectives. Here you will also find questions to consider in embarking on world building—these should prove useful to writers developing any setting but are particularly focused on fantastic or otherworldy settings.

By the end of this book, it is our hope that readers will gain inspiration from—and a renewed appreciation for—the genius of authors who transport us to worlds both familiar and fantastical, using the power of place to illuminate the complexities of the human experience.

Setting the Scene
what's in place?

Setting is the time, location, and physical environment of a narrative. It is important to a writer for seven primary reasons:

ESTABLISHING CONTEXT: Setting grounds a narrative in a specific context, enriching the background culture of the story.

CREATING ATMOSPHERE AND MOOD: The description of the setting helps create the feel and emotion of the story. A dark and stormy mountaintop evokes a very different atmosphere to a sunlit meadow.

INFLUENCING CHARACTERS: Setting can impact characters' behavior, decisions, and development, and can shape their backgrounds, beliefs, and actions. A character from a war-torn country will have different experiences and perspectives than one in a peaceful, prosperous society.

SUPPORTING THE PLOT: Setting can play a direct role in the plot. It can create obstacles and challenges for characters, serve as a catalyst for events, and provide opportunities for action and conflict. For example, an isolated island setting can create tension and drama in a survival story.

ENHANCING IMMERSION: A well-described setting can help make the story more believable and immersive for the reader.

BUILDING SYMBOLISM AND THEME: Settings can symbolize larger ideas and themes within the story. For example, a decaying mansion might symbolisz the decline of a once-great family or society.

REFLECTING INNER STATES: Setting can mirror the internal states of characters. A chaotic, cluttered flat might reflect mental confusion.

A writer can describe a setting in two complementary ways: **MIMESIS** attempts a highly detailed representation of reality, while **IMPRESSIONISM** emphasizes a more subjective and sensory experience of the same reality. Whether you describe your setting in meticulous detail, or only provide essential details and focus more on its 'spirit of place' is up to you, as is your choice of narrator for your story. Whatever your style, your object is **VERISIMILITUDE**: your tale must be believable—*similar to truth*.

Setting can also be a peripheral presence, helping to set a mood with a sunny day, for example. Sometimes, placed right at the core of a narrative, setting can become a vital character of its own, affecting all action, thought and dialogue: think of London in Charles Dickens' *Oliver Twist*, or Emily Brontë's brooding Yorkshire moors in *Wuthering Heights*. Setting is also routinely reimagined—changing a setting but keeping the plot can add an entirely new element to a familiar story. Baz Luhrmann moved Shakespeare's *Romeo and Juliet* to Venice Beach California—Jane Austen's *Emma* moves to an American High school in the classic '90s film *Clueless*.

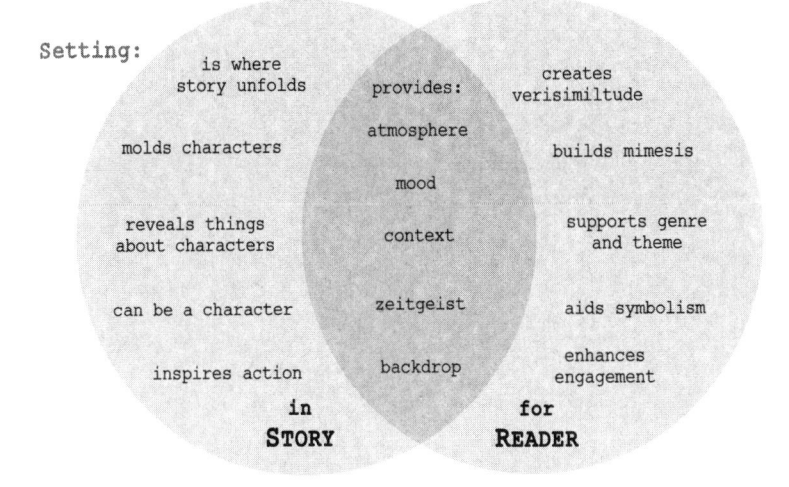

Setting:

in STORY	provides:	for READER
is where story unfolds	atmosphere	creates verisimiltude
molds characters	mood	builds mimesis
reveals things about characters	context	supports genre and theme
can be a character	zeitgeist	aids symbolism
inspires action	backdrop	enhances engagement

Setting & Theme
capturing a zeitgeist

Setting can be highly thematic. In *To Kill a Mockingbird* by Harper Lee, the setting of the racially segregated American South during the 1930s is crucial for exploring themes of racism, justice, and moral growth. In John Steinbeck's *The Grapes of Wrath*, the harsh, oppressive environments of the Dust Bowl and migrant camps highlight themes of poverty, struggle, and social injustice. In *A Bend in the River*, V. S. Naipaul uses the setting of a remote African town to explore themes around the political upheaval, corruption and violence that accompany the end of colonial rule:

> *As I got deeper into Africa — the scrub, the desert, the rocky climb up to the mountains, the lakes, the rain in the afternoons, the mud, and then, on the other, wetter side of the mountains, the fern forests and the gorilla forests — as I got deeper I thought: But this is madness. I am going in the wrong direction.* V. S. Naipaul, A Bend in the River, 1979

Other writers weave more complex relationships between theme and place, such as Tolstoy's 1877 masterpiece *Anna Karenina*:

> *Stepan Arkadyevitch took no part in the country pleasures and occupations. Everything in the country seemed dull and out of joint, deprived of the sense of elegance and refinement that it had in his eyes in the city.* Leo Tolstoy, Anna Karenina, 1877

Themes combine with settings to reflect or interrogate the prevailing zeitgeist or 'spirit of the age': e.g. East *vs* West post 9/11 in Mohsin Hamid's 2006 *The Reluctant Fundamentalist*, or technology, freedom and the rise of facism in Aldous Huxley's 1931 *Brave New World*. Don't underestimate the significance of wider global events when trying to capture a time setting. A useful exercise might be to think about what events are influential in the general mood of our present era and how this manifests on a daily basis.

One of the best zeitgeist-summoning openings is in Charles Dickens' *A Tale of Two Cities*, capturing the response to the French Revolution:

> It was the best of times, it was the worst of times, it was the age of wisdom, it was the age of foolishness, it was the epoch of belief, it was the epoch of incredulity, it was the season of Light, it was the season of Darkness, it was the spring of hope, it was the winter of despair, we had everything before us, we had nothing before us, we were all going direct to Heaven, we were all going direct the other way. Charles Dickens, A Tale of Two Cities, 1859

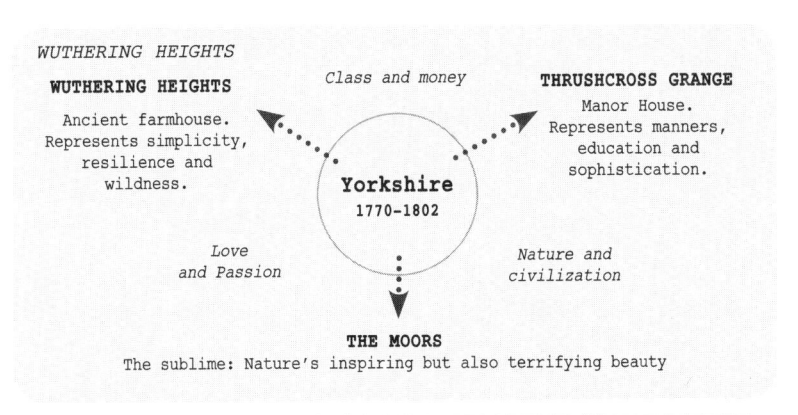

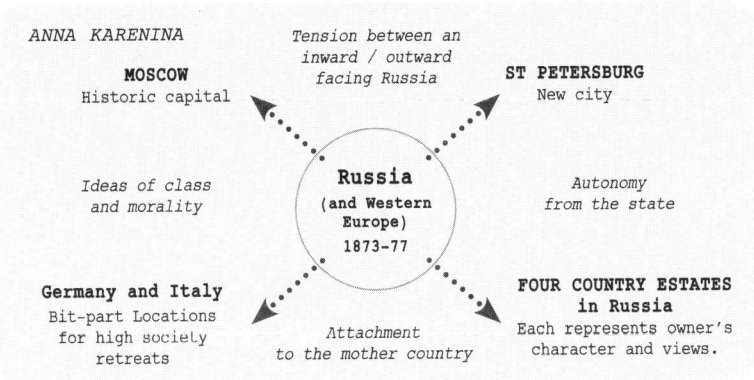

WUTHERING HEIGHTS

WUTHERING HEIGHTS
Ancient farmhouse. Represents simplicity, resilience and wildness.

Class and money

THRUSHCROSS GRANGE
Manor House. Represents manners, education and sophistication.

Yorkshire 1770-1802

Love and Passion

Nature and civilization

THE MOORS
The sublime: Nature's inspiring but also terrifying beauty

ANNA KARENINA

MOSCOW
Historic capital

Tension between an inward / outward facing Russia

ST PETERSBURG
New city

Ideas of class and morality

Russia (and Western Europe) 1873-77

Autonomy from the state

Germany and Italy
Bit-part Locations for high society retreats

Attachment to the mother country

FOUR COUNTRY ESTATES in Russia
Each represents owner's character and views.

CHARACTER & PLACE
home or away

Places inhabit characters just as much as characters inhabit places. We all come from somewhere, somewhere is always home, and those settings have a formative impact on us as individuals. Where we're not at home, we are in alien territory, on the back foot. Whether your character is on familiar or unfamiliar ground can have a powerful effect on the tone of your work.

Bernadino Everisto's *Girl, Woman, Other* opens with protagonist Amma walking *along the promenade of the waterway that bisects her city*, before *the city clogs up with heat and fumes*. Passing the theatre where her play, *The Last Amazon of Dahomey*, will open that night she thinks back:

> *she remembers pouring a pint of beer over the head of a director whose play featured semi-naked black women running around on stage behaving like idiots / before doing a runner into the backstreets of Hammersmith* Bernadino Everisto, Girl, Woman, Other, 2019

London shapes Amma, she in turn shapes aspects of its culture. A free flowing style without full stops or paragraphs (Everisto calls it *fusion fiction*) traces a journey through both mind and city. We get a similar interconnectivity with place in Toni Morrison's 1992 novel *Jazz*, set in Harlem, New York:

> *Daylight slants like a razor cutting the buildings in half. In the top half I see looking faces and it's not easy to tell which are people, which the work of stonemasons. Below is shadow where any blasé thing takes place: clarinets and lovemaking, fists and the voices of sorrowful women. A city like this one makes me dream tall and feel in on things. Hep.*

The tone is again colloquial, the description alive with motion that is both beautiful and violent, it really is a place to *dream tall*. St. Petersburg in the opening of Dostoevsky's *Crime and Punishment* has the opposite effect:

> *The heat in the street was terrible: and the airlessness, the bustle and the plaster, scaffolding, bricks, and dust all about him, and that special Petersburg stench, so familiar to all who are unable to get out of town in summer--all worked painfully upon the young man's already overwrought nerves.* Dostoevsky, Crime and Punishment, 1866

Rodion Raskolnikov, a native of St. Petersburg, has no love for the place—he is alien even at home, setting the scene for his desperate unraveling.

When the environment is challenging, the setting can become a character of its own. *Heat and Dust* follows an Englishwoman in India, her sense of being in an alien setting laying the ground for later tensions:

> *The rest of the time Olivia was alone in her big house with all the doors and windows shut to keep out the heat and dust.* Ruth Prawer Jhabvala, Heat and Dust, 1975

People are different when abroad, excitement can catalyze unusual behaviors and adventures. *Tender is the Night* follows American holidaymakers on the French Riviera, the intoxicating mixture of wealth and travel boiling over into affairs, decadence and murder. The place itself becomes antagonist:

> *In the square, as they came out, a suspended mass of gasoline exhaust cooked slowly in the July sun. It was a terrible thing — unlike pure heat it held no promise of rural escape but suggested only roads choked with the same foul asthma.* F Scott Fitzgerald, Tender is the Night, 1934

```
                    Dressing a Room for Character

Think about a room which you have been in recently which was unfamiliar
to you, what do you remember of it?

    Let's say for example:
1.  That we are in a study in an old house - this already evokes a
    certain image of dark wood and bookcases without us saying it.
2.  Let's put in a case of butterflies and moths, a little ominous.
3.  Dust lies thickly on the bookcase - why is this room unkempt?
4.  The one thing in the room which is not dusty is the drinks cabinet.

The room is dressed, this is more than enough for us to get a good sense
of tone and characterization before we meet the inhabitant ...
```

ATMOSPHERE & MOOD
feeling the vibes

ATMOSPHERE is how a place *feels*. **MOOD** is the emotional response of your reader to what they are reading. Combining these is a dark art. Spoon on atmosphere too thickly and your reader may drown in it; too thinly and your valley, forest, city, castle or spaceship may lack verisimilitude. Create too much mood and your narrative can feel melodramatic; too little and your reader can fail to connect with your characters and events.

Consider the mood created by these contrasting expositions. First, Herman Hesse's opening lines from his novel *Siddhartha*, which transport us to the serenity of ancient India. The atmosphere is dream-like, nurturing:

> *In the shade of the house, in the sunlight on the riverbank where the boats were moored, in the shade of the sal wood and the shade of the fig tree, Siddhartha grew up, the Brahmin's handsome son, the young falcon...* Herman Hesse, Siddhartha, 1922

In Charles Dickens' *Great Expectations*, we get a more sinister, foreboding version of nature as seen through the eyes of both narrator and author:

> *At such a time I found out for certain, that this bleak place overgrown with nettles was the churchyard; and that ... the dark flat wilderness beyond the churchyard, intersected with dykes and mounds and gates, with scattered cattle feeding on it, was the marshes; and that the low leaden line beyond was the river; and that the distant savage lair from which the wind was rushing, was the sea; and that the small bundle of shivers growing afraid of it all and beginning to cry, was Pip.* Great Expectations. 1861

In genres like horror, murder mystery and romance, mood is often front and center, and pathetic fallacy (where human emotions, traits or intentions are attributed to nature, inanimate objects or animals) is more overt. Here is the opening to Shirley Jackson's 1959 novel *The Haunting of Hill House*:

> No live organism can continue for long to exist sanely under conditions of absolute reality; even larks and katydids are supposed, by some, to dream. Hill House, <u>not sane</u>, stood by itself against its hills, <u>holding darkness within</u>; it had stood so for eighty years and might stand for eighty more. Within, walls continued upright, bricks met neatly, floors were firm, and doors were sensibly shut; silence lay steadily against the wood and stone of Hill House, <u>and whatever walked there, walked alone</u>...

If you read this aloud but omit the underlined words the atmosphere is not so eerie. These key details (and the mood clue in the book's name) jolt us out of complacency, contrasting with the more prosaic house descriptors.

Mood can be evoked locally (*as above*) or on a general, macrocosmic level. This can be a particular time and place—London during the blitz, prohibition Chicago—or an attempt to convey zeitgiest (*see p.4*).

> It was in 1590 — winter. Austria was far away from the world, and asleep; it was still the Middle Ages in Austria, and promised to remain so forever.
>
> Mark Twain, The Mysterious Stranger, and Other Stories. 1916

The **TONE**, or style of voice, of author, narrator or character—be it formal, conversational, epic, serious, whimsical, philosophical, humorous, sensual, or mindful—can co-create, support, or be changed by mood. Mood and tone may shift around within a narrative, but if this happens too much, or in too contrasting a manner, the work can feel fragmented.

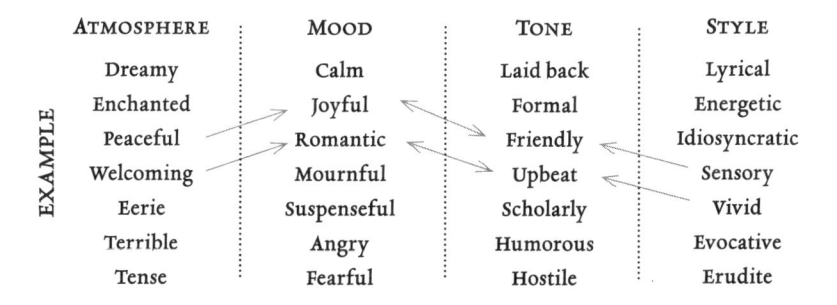

	ATMOSPHERE	MOOD	TONE	STYLE
EXAMPLE	Dreamy	Calm	Laid back	Lyrical
	Enchanted	Joyful	Formal	Energetic
	Peaceful	Romantic	Friendly	Idiosyncratic
	Welcoming	Mournful	Upbeat	Sensory
	Eerie	Suspenseful	Scholarly	Vivid
	Terrible	Angry	Humorous	Evocative
	Tense	Fearful	Hostile	Erudite

DESCRIPTION
plainsong or Baroque

When reading a novel, do you sometimes skip lengthy expositions of setting or do you always read every word and imagine the scene in every detail in your mind's eye? Margaret Atwood defined two extremes for passages of descriptive prose, they were *plainsong* (minimalist) or *Baroque* (elaborated), or somewhere in between.

Many great writers from the 18th and 19th centuries were avid walkers; they experienced the world slowly and described it thus. Here is Thomas Hardy introducing Egdon Heath:

> A Saturday afternoon in November was approaching the time of twilight, and the vast tract of unenclosed wild known as Egdon Heath embrowned itself moment by moment. Overhead the hollow stretch of whitish cloud shutting out the sky was as a tent which had the whole heath for its floor. Thomas Hardy, The Return of the Native, 1878

Hardy continues like this for twelve pages (1481 words) before the first characters show up. His sentences are spacious, ponderous and deliberate. Dickens, a great flaneur (urban walker), while still Baroque, adopts a more breathless style to evoke the chaos of London's Covent Garden market:

> The pavement is already strewed with decayed cabbage-leaves, broken hay-bands, and all the indescribable litter of a vegetable market; men are shouting, carts backing, horses neighing, boys fighting, basket-women talking, piemen expatiating on the excellence of their pastry, and donkeys braying. Charles Dickens, Sketches by Boz, 1836

By contrast, here is one of the masters of the plainsong approach, Ernest Hemingway, opening his 1927 short story *Hills Like White Elephants*:

> The hills across the valley of the Ebro' were long and white. On this side there was no shade and no trees and the station was between two lines of rails in the sun.

Hemingway's style is very matter of fact (very few or no adjectives or literary devices) and very quickly come characters and dialogue. Many contemporary writers adopt a similar approach, but not everyone can do it well, the devil is very much in which detail to draw.

Much description in modern writing includes the presence, or voice, of the describee. Here, character, theme, plot, and setting all merge:

> *I stood watching the shadowy fish slide through the gloom of the mill-pond. They were grey, descendants of the silvery things that had darted away from the monks, in the young days when the valley was lusty.* D.H. Lawrence, The White Peacock, 1913

This is description coloured by the narrator. But Lawrence also knows how to appreciate things as they *are*, be it a city, old gate or wild common:

> The common with the grey leaves dropping from the bushes,
> And the dry, brown grasses,
> And the faint scent of eucalyptus in the twilight... DH Lawrence, The Wild Common, 1909

There are no rules as to how detailed, wordy, referential, or sensory descriptions of setting should be. Sometimes less is more, sometimes more is best. Good writing naturally finds a balance.

Quality of Detail
research and erudition

How do you describe a tree? Do you specify its age, species, leaf-shape, the insects which live on it, or just its general "treeness"? When crafting description, an author must decide what level of *knowledge* to include.

> *The morning air of the pasture turned steadily cooler. Day by day, the bright golden leaves of the birches turned more spotted as the first winds of winter slipped between the withered branches and across the highlands toward the southeast.*
>
> Haruki Murakami, A Wild Sheep Chase, 1982

Note the meticulous nomenclature which Murakami employs—*birches, pasture, highlands, southeasts*—yet there is also space and subtlety in his style.

In a similar vein Bruce Chatwin reveals precise details with ease, here an intimate knowledge of a patch of English countryside:

> *To the east was the River Wye, a silver ribbon snaking through water-meadows, and the whole countryside dotted with white or red-brick farmhouses. A thatched roof made a little patch of yellow in a foam of apple-blossom, and there were gloomy stands of conifers that shrouded the homes of the gentry.* Bruce Chartwin, On the Black Hill, 1982

Chatwin worked in antiques before he became a travel writer and later a novelist. Erudition permeates his fiction:

> *The Ambras Collection, with its Cellini salt-cellar and Montezuma's headdress of quetzal plumes, had survived intact from the sixteenth to the nineteenth centuries when imperial officials, mindful of the revolutionary mob, removed its more spectacular treasures to Vienna. Rudolf's treasures—his mandragoras, his basilisk, his bezoar stone, his unicorn cup, his gold-mounted coco-de-mer, his homunculus in alcohol, his nails from Noah's Ark and the phial of dust from which God created Adam had long ago vanished from Prague.* Bruce Chartwin, Utz, 1988

Genres such as thrillers, crime and science-fiction often rely on the author's ability to provide highly technical details. *The Martian* by Andy Weir, a 2011 take on Defoe's *Robinson Crusoe* of 1712, centers around a lone astronaught, Mark Watney, stranded on Mars. He must use all his ingenuity, scientific knowledge and resourcefulness to survive:

> I have no way to communicate with Hermes or Earth. Everyone thinks I'm dead. I'm in a Hab designed to last thirty-one days. If the oxygenator breaks down, I'll suffocate. If the water reclaimer breaks down, I'll die of thirst. If the Hab breaches, I'll just kind of explode. If none of those things happen, I'll eventually run out of food and starve to death. So yeah. I'm fucked. Andy Weir, The Martian, 2011

Weir did extensive research about what would and wouldn't help Watney survive. Experts conceded that the story is 'just about possible'.

Realistic, informed description of almost any landscape or action (however mundane or mechanical) can help place the reader in the scene. Here a daughter visits her father's workplace, a newspaper print room:

> They watched the curved, freshly cast metal page plates slide in on conveyor rollers to be clamped into place on the cylinders; then after a ringing of bells they watched the presses roll. The steel floor shuddered under their feet, which tickled, and the noise was so overwhelming that they couldn't talk: they could only look at each other and smile and Emily covered her ears with her hands. White streak of newsprint ran in every direction through the machines and finished newspapers came riding out in neat, overlapped abundance. Richard Yates, The Easter Parade, 1976

The writing brims with energy and information, the mundane is transformed into the epic, and it perfectly evokes the sense of awe young children often have for grown ups and their strange worlds.

VISION
the perception of light

Description is strongly anchored in the senses. By engaging the five senses, an author can produce vivid, immersive experiences in the reader's imagination. And since sight is the dominant sense for most of us, details like colors, shapes, sizes and spatial relationships will help readers picture a setting as if they were seeing it themselves. Consider this observational description from Albert Camus:

> Beneath her, the blue-and-white terraces of the Arab town overlapped one another, splattered with the dark-red spots of peppers drying in the sun. A. Camus, L'etranger, 1942

This is **REALISM** exemplified, an accurate sketch with not a word wasted. But Camus is not simply a casual onlooker; there is an appreciation and careful selection of details, and an engagement with the scene. Indeed, alongside visual alertness, a deep curiosity permeates good observational description, especially in novels from the pre-modern era:

> Sunday. The air was full of the smell of flowers, and the buzzing of insects, and the twittering of birds, and there were no people, no wagons, there was no stir of life, nothing going on. The road was mainly a winding path with hoof-prints in it, and now and then a faint trace of wheels on either side in the grass—wheels that apparently had a tire as broad as one's hand. Mark Twain. A Connecticut Yankee in King Arthur's Court, 1889

An easy tone is conjured with simple yet evocative imagery- the narrator is half child, half detective. Thomas Hardy is often cited as a master of sensory description. His 1895 novel *Jude the Obscure* opens with a young Jude in somber spirits:

> A tear rolled from his eye into the depths of the well. The morning was a little foggy, and the boy's breathing unfurled itself as a thicker fog upon the still and heavy air.

Both Hardy and Twain write at the pace of their age. Their powers of observation are well honed and they also see the exotic in the everyday, the beautiful in the seemingly commonplace.

Describing the quality of light is a good thing to master. Practice with sunsets, north light, and full moons over water. This **IMPRESSIONIST** approach is used to good effect by horror writer James Herbert:

> Occasionally the sun broke through and the landscape sparkled, the greens of the meadows taking on a new lustre, the hills in the distance softening to a shimmer; the beech woods lent darker shades while wild flowers added glitter. The Ghosts of Sleath, 1994

The use of light creates a disarmingly idyllic setting, what could go wrong?

Toying with visual perspective, looking at a given setting from a different camera angle, can make description more dynamic. This is especially effective when magnifying, or **BLOWING UP,** significant scenes. The opening to *Enduring Love* is described first from above:

> I see us from two hundred feet up, through the eyes of the buzzard we had watched earlier, soaring, circling, and dipping in the tumult of currents: five men running silently toward the center of a hundred-acre field. I approached from the southeast, with the wind at my back. Ian McEwan, Enduring Love, 1997

Then, the same moment from the ground:

> ... we heard a man's shout. We turned to look across the field and saw the danger. Next thing, I was running toward it.

Sound
harmony, cacophony, & silence

Sounds can be transportive and establish setting with minimal description. Imagine a character undergoing heartbreak during a mundane train announcement, a woodland full of birdsong suddenly falling silent. Sounds can be powerful emotional or memory-based triggers and their use in place of explicit description can turn a scene over to the reader's imagination in a more powerful way than being spoon-fed visual description.

John Hull, in his memoir *On Sight and Insight: A Journey Into the World of Blindness*, hones in on the sound of rain:

> There is a slow, steady drip, drip, drip, and a more rapid cascade, against the background of the pitter-patter of the individual drops on the window pane. These vary in speed as the rainstorm itself ebbs and flows, and some patterns of sounds overtake others, a bit like the music of Steve Reich. I notice now that there are differences in intensity. Here a surface is meeting the full force of the rain but here is a sheltered place. John M. Hull, On Sight and Insight, 2004

More often it is the subtle interplay of different sounds that transports us:

> It was a place full of light and shade; tranquil; it seemed beyond the touch of time; full of silence, full of rustlings— the soft noise of running water that feeds the palms and slips from tree to tree, the quiet call of pigeons, the song of the flute the boy was playing. He was sitting, almost naked, on the trunk of a fallen palm-tree, watching the herd of goats. Andre Gide, The Immoralist, 1902

In the final scene of Quentin Tarantino's first *Kill Bill* movie, Beatrice Kiddo and O-Ren Ishii face off in silence. Snow falls in a Japanese garden as O-Ren silently slips off her shoes. The camera pans out to the two warriors facing one another and a single sound beats out a slow pulse: a

Shishi-odoshi. The knocks of this bamboo water feature echo across the otherwise silent tension of the scene.

Around 600 years earlier, the Gawain poet also recognized the significance of sound in setting in the Middle English poem *Gawain and the Green Knight*. The eponymous knight enters the realm of his adversary in eerie silence before:

> ...he heard on the hillside, from behind a hard rock
> And beyond the brook a blood-chilling noise.
> What! It cannoned through the cliffs as if they might crack,
> like the scream of a scythe being ground on a stone.
> What! It whined and wailed, like a waterwheel.
> What! It rasped and rang, raw on the ear. Gawain and the Green Knight, late 14th-century

Cacophonous sounds can have a disarming effect. A fight scene in Alfred Hitchcock's 1951 film *Strangers on a Train* occurs amidst the clamour of a fun fair; the protagonists grapple, the tune of the carousel accelerates and the cries of delight from the fairgoers rise to frantic screams—a masterly use of sound and setting working on multiple levels. Here, F. Scott Fitzgerald describes a happier sort of cacophony:

> By seven o'clock the orchestra has arrived, no thin five-piece affair, but a whole pitful of oboes and trombones and saxophones and viols and cornets and piccolos, and low and high drums... The bar is in full swing, and floating rounds of cocktails permeate the garden outside, until the air is alive with chatter and laughter, and casual innuendo and introductions forgotten on the spot, and enthusiastic meetings between women who never knew each other's names. F. Scott Fitzgerald, The Great Gatsby, 1925

As well as describing a sound, the language you use can create setting through sound. Lewis Carroll's 1871 *Jabberwocky* poem paints a murky and sinister setting for his fantastical depiction:

> 'Twas brillig, and the slithy toves/ Did gyre and gimble in the wabe: /All mimsy were the borogoves, / And the mome raths outgrabe.

SMELL & TASTE
the instinctual senses

SMELL and taste are deeply instinctual mechanisms for transporting minds to other places, and other times. Places, like people, have distinct smells.

In his 1981 novel, *Midnight's Children*, Salman Rushdie hones in on scent to vividly evoke the lively, chaotic atmosphere of Bombay:

> …the fragrances poured into me: the mournful decaying fumes of animal faeces in the gardens of the Frere Road museum, the pustular body odours of young men in loose pajamas holding hands in Sadar evenings, the knife-sharpness of expectorated betel-nut and the bitter-sweet commingling of betel and opium: 'rocket paans' were sniffed out in the hawker-crowded alleys between Elphin-stone Street and Victoria Road.
>
> Salman Rushdie, Midnight's Children, 1981

Patrick Suskind takes us to task with lip-curling relish for forgetting the stench of eighteenth century France:

> In the period of which we speak, there reigned in the cities a stench barely conceivable to us modern men and women. The streets stank of manure, the courtyards of urine, the stairwells stank of moldering wood and rat droppings, the kitchens of spoiled cabbage and mutton fat; the unaired parlors stank of stale dust, the bedrooms of greasy sheets, damp featherbeds, and the pungently sweet aroma of chamber pots.
>
> Patrick Suskind, Perfume: The Story of a Murderer, 2006

In some ancient form of ourselves, smell remains an early warning system. Roald Dahl uses this to great effect by describing the ominously sweet old woman in his 1959 short story *The Landlady*:

> he caught a whiff of a peculiar smell that seemed to emanate directly from her person. It was not in the least unpleasant, and it reminded him – well, he wasn't quite sure what it reminded him of. Pickled walnuts? New leather? Or was it the corridors of a hospital?

The TASTE of certain foods can also trigger journeys across time and space. The most famous example is the "madeleine moment" in Proust's 1913 *À la recherche du temps perdu*, where the protagonist experiences a rush of childhood memories after tasting a small cake dipped in tea.

Indeed, the near miraculous effect that food and wine may have on mood is often noted by writers:

> As I ate the oysters with their strong taste of the sea and their faint metallic taste that the cold white wine washed away, leaving only the sea taste and the succulent texture, and as I drank their cold liquid from each shell and washed it down with the crisp taste of the wine, I lost the empty feeling and began to be happy and to make plans. Ernest Hemingway, A Moveable Feast, 1964

Goût de terroir, the relationship between taste and place, can inspire writers in a broader sense (*terroir* is an integral part of viticulture where soil type and other local conditions define a wine's character):

> The chocolates had a unique goût de terroir, a flavor that captured the essence of the French countryside. Each truffle, each bonbon, seemed to whisper secrets of the fields, the forests, and the rivers that surrounded the village. Chocolat, Joanne Harriss, 1999

Both taste and smell are often used in their metaphorical sense too:

> What's that smell in this room? Didn't you notice it, Brick? Didn't you notice a powerful and obnoxious odor of mendacity in this room? There ain't nothin' more powerful than the odor of mendacity. You can smell it. It smells like death.
>
> Tennessee Williams, Cat on a Hot Tin Roof, 1955

Touch & Feeling
and overlapping senses

TOUCH is often overlooked in the art of description, but it is ever-present nevertheless. Feel this book in your hands. Enter a shopping mall and notice the cool blast of air conditioning. Lie on a beach and enjoy the delicious sensation of warm sun and drying salt on skin.

Touch is often described in fiction at heightened moments where characters suddenly become aware of their bodies, as here in the beautifully written final scene of Kate Chopin's *The Awakening*:

> *she cast the unpleasant, pricking garments from her, and for the first time in her life she stood naked in the open air, at the mercy of the sun, the breeze that beat upon her, and the waves that invited her. […] The foamy wavelets curled up to her white feet, and coiled like serpents about her ankles. She walked out. The water was chill, but she walked on. The water was deep, but she lifted her white body and reached out with a long, sweeping stroke. The touch of the sea is sensuous, enfolding the body in its soft, close embrace.* Kate Chopin, The Awakening, 1898

Touch is closely related to texture. Things can be rough, smooth, soft, hard, fuzzy, slippery, sticky, gritty, bumpy, spongey, prickly, crinkly, etc. Here, Aimee Nezhukumatathil uses touch to accentuate what is real:

> *If by real you mean as real as a shark tooth stuck*
> *in your heel, the wetness of a finished lollipop stick,*
> *the surprise of a thumbtack in your purse—*
> *then Yes, every last page is true, every nuance,*
> *bit, and bite …* Aimee Nezhukumatathil, extract from Are All the Break-Ups in Your Poems Real, 2011

Certain people, known as **SYNAESTHETES**, experience colors when listening to music, see shapes when smelling certain scents, or perceive tastes when looking at words—perceptual crossovers which can inspire highly original wordplay. Vladimir Nabokov was a mild colour synaesthete; he is noted for his rich use of imagery and spine tingling depth of thought:

> *The grayness of rain would soon engulf everything. He felt a first kiss on his bald spot and walked back to the woods and widowhood.* Vladimir Nabokov, Transparent Things, 1972

Compare that with this contemporary description of a Spanish red wine:

> *Medium body, fine-grained and very silky tannins for a wine of almost 10 years of age, bright and transparent acidity and a long, very spicy finish. Like going back in time and touching an ornate tapestry. The texture is mesmerizing.*

A different kind of feeling, the SIXTH SENSE, can also be invoked to enrich setting, often the feeling that things aren't quite as they should be:

> *I feel perfectly awful! When are we going home?" Miranda was looking at her so strangely, almost as if she wasn't seeing her. When Edith repeated the question more loudly, she simply turned her back and began walking away up the rise, the other two following a little way behind. Well, hardly walking — sliding over the stones on their bare feet as if they were on a drawing-room carpet...* Joan Lindsay, Picnic at Hanging Rock, 1967

For maximum effect, all six senses can be described in a single passage. But so too, the apparent absence, or extreme subtlety, of feeling can also be described by the sensitive writer. As silence is to noise, so stillness is to movement:

> *And now (how shall I describe it?), now all was still. Still, as when some pain ceases. A peculiarly perceptible, prickling stillness, as if a wound were healing.*
>
> Rainer Maria Rilke, Journal of My Other Self, 1910

Recognisable Settings
fictional stories in factual places

What kind of setting might an author choose for their story? Most opt for a RECOGNIZABLE SETTING, somewhere already familiar to the reader, already laden with cultural, historical and social connotations primed to enhance the themes and narrative of the work (*for* ALTERED *or* FANTASY SETTINGS, *see pages 52-55*). With the culture, language and even the cuisine of the setting already familiar to the reader, the story unfolds in a real and shared realm, which 'anchors' the text and enhances verisimilitude:

> We came then near the river. We spent a long time walking about the noisy streets flanked by high stone walls … We pleased ourselves with the spectacle of Dublin's commerce — the barges signalled from far away by their curls of woolly smoke, the brown fishing fleet beyond Ringsend, the big white sailing-vessel which was being discharged on the opposite quay. James Joyce, Dubliners, 1914

One benefit of using recognizable settings is that writers can rely on the prior knowledge of the reader to imagine many of the physical details.

The Louvre scenes in Dan Brown's *Da Vinci Code* evoke images already established in the mind of the reader—the French capital's stylish and carefully curated museum, a place of hushed voices in crowded rooms. A few light touch descriptors are all that is required:

> Renowned curator Jacques Saunière staggered through the vaulted archway of the museum's Grand Gallery. He lunged for the nearest painting he could see, a Caravaggio. Dan Brown, The Da Vinci Code, 2003

Familiar objects too, require little or no description:

> They followed her into the dining-parlour. It was a large, well-proportioned room, handsomely fitted up. Elizabeth, after slightly surveying it, went to a window to

enjoy its prospect. The hill, crowned with wood, from which they had descended, receiving increased abruptness from the distance, was a beautiful object"

Jane Austen, Pride and Prejudice, 1813

A huge industry has sprung up around literary locations. Tourists can visit Sherlock Holmes' Baker Street home (the fictional world bleeding in to the real here) while the Georgian streets of Bath play host to Jane Austen fans. Iconic landmarks feature in many novels. Roland Barthes explored this in an essay on the Eiffel Tower, perhaps the ultimate symbol of 'Frenchness'—whatever that might mean. In Jean Cocteau's play *Les Maries de la Tour Eiffel*, set during a wedding party on its first floor:

> *… so dominant is the role of the Eiffel Tower in this play, in fact, that the Tower itself may be considered the central character. Far from being a banal, static setting for the action, the tower stands as a prominent backdrop without which the play and all its action would lose significance.* The French Review, Vol. 73, No. 6, May, 2000

In *The Goldfinch*, Donna Tartt sets a section of her novel in the familiar surrounds of seedy Las Vegas—the perfect place for protagonist Theo to find himself *high and lying on the shag carpet in Vegas laughing at the ceiling fan*.

Contrasting Settings
country mouse and town mouse

Narratives often focus on two distinct locations, a dichotomy which can be rich in symbolic resonance, supporting divergent aspects of theme, plot, character and mood. If these settings exist simultaneously within the narrative they may be termed **PARALLEL LOCATIONS**.

Americanah, a 2013 novel by Chimamanda Ngozi Adichie, follows the lives of Ifemelu and Obinze, young lovers in Nigeria separated when Ifemelu moves to the United States to attend university. The result is a rich exploration of cultural difference and belonging:

> I came from a country where race was not an issue; I did not think of myself as black and I only became black when I came to America. Chimamanda Ngozi Adichie, *Americanah*, 2013

The two settings in his 1859 *A Tale of Two Cities* allows Charles Dickens to craft concurrent storylines (*opposite*), which converge in the novel's final section when key London-based characters find themselves in Paris.

George Orwell's 1933 *Down and Out in Paris and London* recounts his experiences living among impoverished and marginalized communities. The locations are presented sequentially (he first lives in London then Paris). It is a masterly study in **SOCIO-GEOGRAPHY** and character:

> Paris is a very convenient place to be ill in. You can do without heating and almost without food, and still live, which is more than you can say for London.

Sometimes it is not locations that are contrasted but emotions. In Rudyard Kipling's 1890 *Without Benefit of Clergy*, the perfect happiness of lovers Holden and Ameera is juxtaposed with a plague-infested city:

> In the gray dawn they saw the dead borne out through the city gates, each litter with its own little knot of mourners. Wherefore they kissed each other and shivered.

In his 2009 science fiction novel *The City & The City*, China Miéville presents two cities, Besźel and Ul Qoma, which coexist in the same physical space but are perceived as separate entities by their inhabitants, who are trained from birth to "unsee" the other. This intricate setting explores themes of state power, perception, and the nature of reality:

> Those most dedicated to the perforation of the boundary between Besźel and Ul Qoma had to observe it most carefully. If I or one of my friends were to have a moment's failure of unseeing (and who did not do that? who failed to fail to see, sometimes?), so long as it was not flaunted or indulged in, we should not be in danger. If I were to glance a second or two on some attractive passerby in Ul Qoma, if I were to silently enjoy the skyline of the two cities together, be irritated by the noise of an Ul Qoman train, I would not be taken.

LONDON	THEMES	PARIS
Rule of law. Injustice addressed through compassion	justice vengeance sacrifice redemption	Rule of the mob. Injustice addressed through chaos
Lucie Manette	**CHARACTERS** contrasted	Madame Defarge
Charles Darnay Sydney Carton	move between	Charles Darnay Sydney Carton
Focus on personal: relationships and struggles	**PLOT** complementary	Focus on action: revolution, white terror, escape
haven	**ROLE** contrasting	crucible
relatively tranquil, stable, nervous, restrained	**MOOD** contrasting	intense, ominous, charged with revolutionary fervor

PARALLEL SETTINGS in A TALE OF TWO CITIES

Past Settings
they do things differently there

Time is just as important to setting as place. Setting a story in the PAST allows an author to immerse their readers in the sands of time and creates a sense of escapism. As the opening line of L. P. Hartley's 1953 novel *The Go-Between* reminds us:

> *The past is a foreign country: they do things differently there.*

Many writers turn to the RECENT PAST, or their childhood. Douglas Stuart's 2020 novel *Shuggie Bain* tells the story of a boy growing up in poverty-stricken Glasgow with his alcoholic mother, capturing the harsh realities of his own early life in a decimated mining town.

> *Lizzie tried to quietly burst the cellophane on a new cigarette packet. The other women were hawkish, growing sick of smoking harsh rollies and picking tobacco off the ends of their tongues. Lizzie sniffed, "I thought we were smoking our own?" But it was like eating ham hock in front of a pack of strays; they would give her no peace. She grudgingly passed around the fresh pack, and everyone lit up, enjoying the luxury of a manufactured cigarette....The air in the room grew hot and curdled again as the smoke swirled and danced with the paisley wallpaper.* Douglass Stuart, Shuggie Bain, 2020

The MIDDLE PAST is further back. The *Iliad* and the *Odyssey* are set around the 12th century BC, but were composed by Homer in the 8th century BC. The oldest known English tale, *Beowulf*, was set in the 6th century, and composed in England between the 7th and 10th centuries. Both use the mists of time to conjure monsters. Today, it is populated with medieval detectives (e.g. Ellis Peters' Brother Cadfael and C. J. Sansom's Shardlake) and swashbucking adventurers (e.g. Patrick O'Brian's Jack Aubrey and Bernard Cornwell's Uhtred of Bebbanburg). Works like this are not easy to pull off. Hilary Mantel's meticulous research for her works of historical fiction is renowned, she advises that:

> The writer of history is a walking anachronism, a displaced person, using today's techniques to try to know things about yesterday that yesterday didn't know itself. He must try to work authentically, hearing the words of the past, but communicating in a language the present understands. Hilary Mantel, Reith Lectures, 2017

Mantel notes that historical records are useful sources, but folk tales, myths and rumors can also help to capture the zeitgeist. She advises using 'tags' to signpost the era, rather than emulating the language of the past precisely:

> She bawls for her husband: "Morgan Williams!" She rotates on the spot, eyes wild, face flushed from the oven's heat. "Take this tray, <u>body of God</u>, where are you all?" Hilary Mantel, Wolf Hall, 2017

Another example can be found in Susan Hill's *The Woman in Black*—written in 1983 and set eighty years earlier:

> the fog, the thickest of London peasoupers...
> had hemmed us in on all sides since dawn –

'Peasoupers', is a historical breadcrumb providing enough to capture the time in otherwise accessible modern narration.

The ANCIENT PAST is even less familiar. Robert Harris's electrifying *Cicero Trilogy* benefits from the huge volume of research that exists on the rise and fall of the Roman Empire, while works like Madeline Miller's 2018 *Circe* reimagine the ancient Greek MYTHIC PAST for the modern age.

Present Settings
familiar and urgent

The majority of bestselling fiction is set in the author's PRESENT. Stories set in the here-and-now, with real-world locations and characters who look and talk like us, hold a mirror to our lives and times. When a book successfully addresses current social, political, environmental or cultural issues and trends the reader engagement can be intense.

A present-day setting also requires less effort in exposition, since we already all share (to some extent) the same cultural and physical landscape. The challenge is verisimilitude; thus era-specific details, like image and communications technologies and their paraphernalia, are often blended into the prose. Here is Raymond Chandler, writing in 1939:

> *I went back to the boulevard. I found a phone book and discovered that Geiger lived on Laverne Terrace, a street off Laurel Canyon Boulevard. … I ran back to my car through heavy rain. Then I opened the packet. I knew what was inside it. A heavy book, full of photographs. They made me feel sick. The worst pornography I had ever seen.* Raymond Chandler, The Big Sleep, 1939

Sally Rooney achieves the same thing with an uncluttered immediacy:

> *A woman sat in a hotel bar, watching the door. Her appearance was neat and tidy: white blouse, fair hair tucked behind her ears. She glanced at the screen of her phone, on which was displayed a messaging interface, and then looked back at the door again. It was late March, the bar was quiet, and outside the window to her right the sun was beginning to set over the Atlantic.* Sally Rooney, Beautiful World, Where Are You, 2021

Technology evolves quickly, so keep any such description vague, but remember that digital communication is now a part of most people's daily lives:

Just like early novels drew on letter-writing, it seems natural to me that contemporary novels would draw on emails and instant messaging, because those are the predominant forms of communicative text now. Sally Rooney, 2021

Contemporary settings are often used to reflect the world *through the glass, darkly,* drawing attention to unpleasant aspects of society. Fiction set in the present can create empathy in a way that real life accounts, oddly, cannot. John Steinbeck, in his 1938 article *Starvation Under the Orange Trees*, voices his dismay that starvation in 1930s California in is not acted upon:

Is it possible that this state is so stupid, so vicious and so greedy that it cannot feed and clothe the men and women who help to make it the richest area in the world? Must the hunger become anger and the anger fury before anything will be done?

This work is far less well known than his 1939 novel *The Grapes of Wrath* in which he addresses the same issues. Steinbeck and other writers with a strong social conscience follow Leo Tolstoy's assertion: that a novel *must* include within its thematic scope the most pressing issues of the times.

In Richard Powers' novel *The Overstory*, character Patricia Westerford summarises the big issue of *our* times:

Honduran rosewood. Hinton's oak in Mexico. St. Helena gumwood. Cedars from the Cape of Good Hope. Twenty species of monster kauri, ten feet thick and clear of branches for a hundred feet and more. An alerce in southern Chile, older than the Bible but still putting forth seeds. Half the species in Australia, southern China, a belt across Africa. The alien life-forms of Madagascar that occur nowhere else on the planet. Saltwater mangroves — marine nurseries and the coasts' protectors — disappearing in a hundred countries. Borneo, Papua New Guinea, the Moluccas, Sumatra: the most productive ecosystems on Earth, giving way to oil palm plantations.

Richard Powers, The Overstory, 2021

Future Settings
same same but different

Setting a narrative in the **FUTURE** unshackles the imagination for writer and reader alike. Most such stories are in the domain of **SCIENCE FICTION**, a subgenre of **SPECULATIVE FICTION**. They allow authors to ask "what if..." and extrapolate future worlds from the present, the degree of change depending on how far into the future the tale is set. Many of the great dystopian writers of the late 19th and 20th centuries chose the not-too-distant future. Ray Bradbury, in his 1950 short story *There Will Come Soft Rains,* jumps only 76 years, predicting improved analog technology:

> In the living room the voice-clock sang ... "Today is Mr. Featherstone's birthday. Today is the anniversary of Tilita's marriage. Insurance is payable, as are the water, gas, and light bills." Somewhere in the walls, relays clicked, memory tapes glided under electric eyes. Ray Bradbury, There Will Come Soft Rains, 1950

Others writers of that era chose much greater time spans:

> The various Bureaux of Propaganda and the College of Emotional Engineering were housed in a single sixty-story building in Fleet Street. Aldous Huxley, Brave New World, 1932

Huxley's 500-year jump requires significant advances in technology and shifts in moral compass. H. G. Wells, a trained biologist (his first published works were biology textbooks), imagines the results of human evolution (and devolution) a billion years in the future in his 1895 *The Time Machine*:

> I saw that, quite near, what I had taken to be a reddish mass of rock was moving slowly towards me. Then I saw the thing was really a monstrous crab-like creature. Can you imagine a crab as large as yonder table, with its many legs moving slowly and uncertainly, its big claws swaying, its long antennae, like carters' whips, waving and feeling, and its stalked eyes gleaming at you on either side of its metallic front?

Note how these narratives occur in altered but familiar settings, utilizing the UNCANNY for reflection and relatability. Ballard's opening chapter in his climate novel *The Drowned World* is entitled 'On the Beach at the Ritz':

> Soon it would be too hot. Looking out from the hotel balcony shortly after eight o'clock, Kerans watched the sun rise behind the dense groves of giant gymnosperms crowding over the roofs of the abandoned department stores four hundred yards away on the east side of the lagoon. J.G. Ballard, The Drowned World, 1962

Many future works reflect contemporary anxieties. Orwell's 1949 masterpiece *1984* explores totalitarianism, Bradbury's *There Will Come Soft Rains* the fear of nuclear technology, John Wyndham's *The Day of the Triffids* the genetic alteration of crops, Richard Matheson's 1954 *I am Legend* viral infection in 1976, and Shirow's 1989 *The Ghost in the Shell* 21st century technological body modification blurring the lines between human and cyborg.

Concerns about robots, hacks, aliens, mutations, immortality and the nature of reality will permeate science fiction writing for some time yet:

> Ill-focused swirls of information raced through this foreign void, similar in nature to the Ly-cilph's own memory facility. They were separate entities, it was sure, though they continually mingled themselves, interpenetrating then diverging. The Ly-cilph observed the alien mentalities cluster around the boundary zone of its identity focus. Delicate wisps of radiation stroked it, bringing a multitude of impossibly jumbled images. It assembled a standardized identity and interpretation message and broadcast it on the same radiation bands they were using. Horrifyingly, instead of responding, the aliens penetrated its boundary. Peter F. Hamilton, The Reality Dysfunction, 1996

```
What if? ... The police can anticipate crimes before they happen (MINORITY
REPORT). Humans travel by air in flying cars (BLADE RUNNER). Earth faces destruction
    by extra terrestrials (WAR OF THE WORLDS, ETC). Human emotions are surpressed,
    happiness is induced by drugs (BRAVE NEW WORLD, ETC). Men become infertile (CHILDREN OF
MEN). All our thoughts and actions are observed by the state (1984). Time travel
is possible (BACK TO THE FUTURE, ETC). London becomes a tropical swamp (THE DROWNED WORLD).
        One house survives after a nuclear bomb (THERE WILL COME SOFT RAINS).
```

Multi-Temporal
now, then and tomorrow

A literary work does not have to keep a consistent setting in time. Many of us have had moments in old buildings where we placed a hand on a wall and imagined events down the ages. Toying with time allows writers to explore questions of universal human nature, causality and coincidence, the hundreds of forking paths opened up by decisions in the past which have led to a current moment.

Tom Stoppard's 2020 play *Leopoldstadt* plays on this idea, staging the Viennese drawing room of a wealthy Jewish family over 50 years:

> 1899: *A hopeful and happy family gather for Christmas, well integrated in society.*
> 1900: *The family gather for Passover Seder, relationship tensions bubble.*
> 1924: *The family gather for a bris. The 'Great War' took its toll. Clouds gather.*
> 1938: *The family are discussing visas and escape plans when Nazi officers burst in.*
> 1955: *Family members who survived the Holocaust gather in the former home.*

Other writers intertwine different times. *The Chymical Wedding* by Lindsay Clarke is set both in 19th-century England (detailing three characters' adventures in alchemy) and in the 20th century (three other characters studying the lives of the first), using alternating chapters:

> *She lifted a hand as though to fend off my voice. Then - it might have been an intrusion from another century - a car passed down the lane outside, its headlights swooping through the window, travelling across the ceiling.* Lindsay Clarke, The Chymical Wedding, 1989

In *The Invisible Life of Addie LaRue*, fantasy writer V. E. Schwab flashes her immortal protagonist between present day New York City and Addie's French childhood in 1714, and her travels over the 300 years inbetween. **FLASHBACKS** and **FLASHFORWARDS** are common ways to present multiplicity in time and space (*see sister book Narrative Devices*).

In *Orlando: A Biography*, 1928, Virginia Woolf describes the adventures of a poet who changes sex from man to woman and lives for centuries, meeting key figures of English literary history. In his 1998 tribute to Virginia Woolf, *The Hours*, author Michael Cunningham weaves together three timelines, that of Woolf herself (in 1923), Laura Brown (who is reading Mrs. Dalloway in 1949) and Clarissa Vaughan (in 1999 New York):

> *Laura Brown is trying to lose herself. No, that's not it exactly — she is trying to keep herself by gaining entry into a parallel world. She lays the book face down on her chest. Already her bedroom (no, their bedroom) feels more densely inhabited, more actual, because a character named Mrs. Dalloway is on her way to buy flowers.*
>
> Michael Cunningham, *The Hours*, 1998

In his 1969 anti-war novel *Slaughterhouse-Five* Kurt Vonnegut utilizes a non-linear, non-chronological description of events. David Mitchell experiments with time in his 2004 *Cloud Atlas*, which has huge spatial and temporal reach, charting the reincarnation of one soul across six selves, from the South Pacific in 1850 to post-apocalyptic Hawaii and back again, In an interview with BBC *Bookclub*, Mitchell explained his method:

> *All of the main characters, except one, are reincarnations of the same soul in different bodies throughout the novel identified by a birthmark... that's just a symbol really of the universality of human nature. The title... refers to the ever changing manifestations of the Atlas, which is the fixed human nature which is always thus and ever shall be. So the book's theme is predacity, the way individuals prey on individuals, groups on groups, nations on nations, tribes on tribes. So I just take this theme and in a sense reincarnate that theme in another context.* David Mitchell

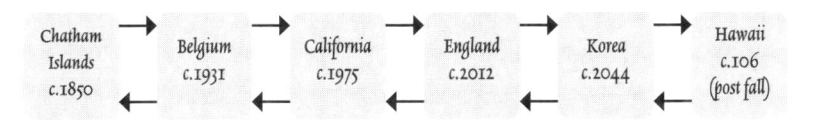

Chatham Islands c.1850 → Belgium c.1931 → California c.1975 → England c.2012 → Korea c.2044 → Hawaii c.106 (post fall)

The Seasons
spring, summer, autumn, winter

In the world's temperate zones, harnessing the power and magic of the four seasons is an age-old component of storytelling. Seasons contain implied meaning (*see opposite*), provide universally understood context, and are often characters in their own right, with positive and negative aspects, as seen here in Oscar Wilde's *The Selfish Giant*:

> But the Spring never came, nor the Summer. The Autumn gave golden fruit to every garden, but to the Giant's garden she gave none. "He is too selfish," she said. So it was always Winter there, and the North Wind, and the Hail, and the Frost, and the Snow danced about through the trees. Oscar Wilde, The Selfish Giant, 1888

SPRING is the fast changing season of new beginnings, birth, hope, youth and innocence. In *As You Like It*, two pages sing a song:

> It was a lover and his lass / With a hey, and a ho, and a hey nonino / That o'er the green cornfield did pass / In springtime, the only pretty ring time / When birds do sing, hey ding a ding, ding / Sweet lovers love the spring. Shakespeare, As You Like It, 1599

SUMMER brings comfort, warmth, and long languid days in the sun:

> In early June the world of leaf and blade and flowers explodes, and every sunset is different. John Steinbeck, The Winter of Our Discontent

But it can also be dangerous. Oppressive heat is a familiar theme in creative works, often the driver of conflict and tension. In *The Talented Mr Ripley* and *A Streetcar Named Desire*, it foreshadows violence. In Chekhov's short story *The Huntsman*, 1885, it frames a strange and depressing encounter:

> 'A sultry, stifling midday. Not a cloudlet in the sky.... The sun-baked grass had a disconsolate, hopeless look: even if there were rain it could never be green again.

AUTUMN is the season of harvest, change, reflection, and the quickening which precedes the cold. John Keats personified it as a drowsy figure:

> *Sometimes whoever seeks abroad may find*
> *Thee sitting careless on a granary floor,*
> *Thy hair soft-lifted by the winnowing wind[...]*
> *Or by a cyder-press, with patient look,*
> *Thou watchest the last oozings hours by hours.*   John Keats, Ode to Autumn, 1820

WINTER is usually associated with darkness and struggle, *Beowulf* tells us that the Grendel has haunted the hall of Heorot for *twelve winters*. It can also evoke stillness, reflection and gathering around a warming fire. Some writers play on the season when the reader is intended to read the work. *The Dark is Rising*, a children's book by Susan Cooper, has also become a cult reading classic in the winter months, with readers beginning on Midwinter's eve (20th December), following the chronology of the narrative by reading a chapter a day until Twelfth Night.

Subverting expectations of the seasons can present them from a new perspective, T.S. Eliot's *The Wasteland* opens telling us that *April is the cruellest month*, an twist on the *Canterbury Tales* Prologue, where it brings new life:

> *Whan that April with his showres soote / The droughte of March hath perced to the roote / And bathed every veine in swich licour.*   Chaucer, Canterbury Tales, 1392

In tropical climates things are very different. Gradually changing seasons give way to dramatic contrasts—wet vs dry seasons, tropical storms.

SPRING	SUMMER	AUTUMN	WINTER
Birth	Youth	Change	Death
Hope	Innocence	Maturity	Desperation
Renewal	Happiness	Abundance	Hardship
Reawakening	Decadence	Harvest	Stillness
Sacrifice	Oppression	Decay	Hibernation
Birth to teens	Early adulthood	Late adulthood	Final Years

THE WEATHER
sun shine, wind blow, rain fall, flowers grow

Making wild thunderstorms, oppressive heat, or bitter cold leap off the page without resorting to cliché is no easy task. The *Gigantic Cinema*, an anthology of weather-based writing, describes *the weather's play-like control of our attention, on the stage of the day*. The title is from a Virginia Woolf essay, *On Being Ill*. She lies recumbent, staring straight up at the drama above:

> *… this incessant making up of shapes and casting them down, this buffeting of clouds together, and drawing vast trains of ships and wagons from North to South, this incessant ringing up and down of curtains of light and shade, this interminable experiment with gold shafts and blue shadows, with veiling the sun and unveiling it, with making rock ramparts and wafting them away … Ought not some one to write to The Times? Use should be made of it. One should not let this gigantic cinema play perpetually to an empty house.* Virginia Woolf, On Being Ill, 1925

Weather can be awe-inspiring, as above, or harnessed to create mood. Symbolism, personification, anthropomorphism, and pathetic fallacy are routinely deployed to this effect. In Disney films, dark clouds gather when danger is afoot, thunder signals desperation; rain can represent alienation (*Snow White*) or renewal, washing away the past (*The Lion King*).

Film adaptions of Mary Shelley's *Frankenstein* often depict the creation of the creature during a great lightning storm, but in the novel rain only patters balefully at the window. Instead, Shelley first uses the device in Chapter 6, when creator beholds creation for the very first time:

> *… the darkness and storm increased every minute, and the thunder burst with a terrific crash over my head … A flash of lightning illuminated the object, and discovered its shape plainly to me; its gigantic stature, and the deformity of its aspect more hideous than belongs to humanity …* Mary Shelley, Frankenstein, 1818

Wind embodies disturbance and change. Anyone who has ever taught in a school knows that a windy day is one to brace for! Sappho wrote over 2000 years ago that *Eros shook my / mind like a mountain wind falling on oak trees*. In Joanne Harris' novel *Chocolat*, wind helps to set both scene and tone:

> *And besides, the wind, the carnival wind, was still blowing, bringing with it the dim scent of grease and cotton candy and gunpowder, the hot sharp scents of the changing seasons, making the palms itch and the heart beat faster.... For a time, then, we stay. For a time. Till the wind changes.* Joanne Harris, Chocolat, 1999

Snow is another matter. It can be beautiful: *You know how the snow glistens at night when the moon shines* writes Fyodor Dostoevsky in *The Brothers Karamazov*, 1880; but it can also be quietly smothering:

> *It had begun to snow again. He watched sleepily the flakes, silver and dark, falling obliquely against the lamplight. His soul swooned slowly as he heard the snow falling faintly through the universe and faintly falling, like the descent of their last end upon all the living and the dead.* James Joyce, Dubliners, 1914

As for sunshine, its light, its heat, its symbolism, here is Tolstoy:

> *He stepped down, trying not to look long at her, as if she were the sun, yet he saw her, like the sun, even without looking.* Leo Tolstoy, Anna Karenina, 1873

You can subvert meteorological expectations: a joyous moment in the midst of a storm, or a balmy summer's evening punctuated by a murder. Contextual factors, housing, affluence, vocation, age, and temperament, may also affect how your characters interact with weather. As Mark Twain notes so well, weather is a *literary speciality*.

Sublime Earth
nature, and isolated settings

Of the SUBLIME, Roman writer Longinus declares in 100CE that:

> *… our soul is uplifted by the true sublime; it takes a proud flight, and is filled with joy and vaunting, as though it had itself produced what it has heard.*

The term now has a narrower meaning, as something exquisitely beautiful, but in its true sense the sublime setting is far more powerful; it is *awful*—a place which inspires awe. Edmund Burke's 1757 *A Philosophical Enquiry into the Origin of our Ideas of the Sublime and Beautiful* tells us that:

> *Whatever is fitted in any sort to excite the ideas of pain, and danger, that is to say, whatever is in any sort terrible, or is conversant about terrible objects, or operates in a manner analogous to terror, is a source of the sublime; that is, it is productive of the strongest emotion which the mind is capable of feeling… The passion caused by the great and the sublime in nature, when those causes operate most powerfully, is Astonishment; and astonishment is that state of the soul, in which all its motions are suspended, with some degree of horror.* Edmund Burke, 1757

Sublime settings are often extreme: perhaps a high cliff edge, a tumultuous ocean, a view over an endless forest, a vast canyon, a galaxy. In *The Snow Leopard*, Peter Matthiessen finds it in the mountains:

> *The sun is roaring, it fills to bursting each crystal of snow. I flush with feeling, moved beyond my comprehension, and once again, the warm tears freeze upon my face. These rocks and mountains, all this matter, the snow itself, the air- the earth is ringing. All is moving, full of power, full of light.* Peter Matthiessen, The Snow Leopard, 1978

The sublime can be described in microcosm, e.g. William Blake's illustration of the soul of a flea, or on a vast scale, such as the wonder and horror of a urban sprawl seen from the air.

ISOLATED SETTINGS in nature, with fewer characters to juggle than a cosmopolitan equivalent, allow a writer to focus on core details. In Michael Punke's survivalist revenge novel *The Revenant*, protagonist Hugh Glass, injured and abandoned in the wilds of America, expresses the sublime:

> *His awe of the mountains grew in the days that followed, as the Yellowstone River led him nearer and nearer. Their great mass was a marker, a benchmark fixed against time itself. Others might feel disquiet at the notion of something so much larger than themselves. But for Glass, there was a sense of sacrament that flowed from the mountains like a font, an immortality that made his quotidian pains seem inconsequential.* The Revenant, 2002

ISLANDS are the ultimate expression of natural remoteness. Before Defoe's *Robinson Crusoe*, Shakespeare used them in *Twelfth Night* (Sicily) and *The Tempest* (fictional) where Caliban tells Stephano and Trinculo to:

> *Be not afeard; The isle is full of noises / Sounds, and sweet airs, that give delight, and hurt not. / Sometimes a thousand twangling instruments / Will hum about mine ears and sometimes voices ...* William Shakespeare, The Tempest, 1611

Not only are islands removed from 'civilization' they can be enchanted 'other worlds'. Jonathan Swift made use of this in his fantastical *Gulliver's Travels*, 1726, as did Yann Martel in his 2001 novel *Life of Pi*.

DESERTS (and the sea) are often metaphors for trial, survival and epiphany. Characters typically face deprivation and hardship in the barren landscape. Antoine de Saint-Exupéry's *Little Prince* sums it up beautifully:

> *I looked across the ridges of sand that were stretched out before us in the moonlight.*
> *"The desert is beautiful," the little prince added.*
> *And that was true. I have always loved the desert. One sits down on a desert sand dune, sees nothing, hears nothing. Yet through the silence something throbs, and gleams ...*
> *"What makes the desert beautiful," said the little prince, "is that somewhere it hides a well ..."* Antoine de Saint-Exupéry, 1943

Above and Below
air, space, underground, underwater

Although most narratives are set on the surface of the Earth, others are set far above or below it. *Catch-22* by Jospeh Heller is set during World War II with much of the action in the AIR. In his 1932 novel *Night Flight*, Antoine de Saint-Exupéry describes airmail pilot Fabien heading into trouble:

> Now the Patagonia mail was entering the storm and Fabien abandoned all idea of the circumventing it; it was too widespread for that, he reckoned, for the vista of lightning-flashes led far inland, exposing battlement on battlement of clouds. He decided to try passing below it, ready to beat a retreat if things took a bad turn.

SPACE as a setting is even further removed from the familiar, and allows the writer to toy with new worlds and life forms, either terrifyingly, as in the 1979 film *Alien*, or playfully as in *The Hitchhiker's Guide to the Galaxy*:

> On this particular Thursday, something was moving quietly through the ionosphere many miles above the surface of the planet; several somethings in fact, several dozen huge yellow chunky slablike somethings, huge as office blocks, silent as birds. They soared with ease, basking in electromagnetic rays from the star Sol, biding their time, grouping, preparing. Douglas Adams, The Hitchhiker's Guide to the Galaxy, 1979

Jules Verne wrote groudbreaking stories set both in space and UNDER THE SEA, such as *From the Earth to the Moon* (1865) and *Twenty Thousand Leagues Under the Seas* (1870). In the 19th century, the two were equally distant and dangerous places, but also liberating too, as Verne's sub-aquatic adventurer Captain Nemo explains:

> The sea doesn't belong to tyrants. On its surface they can still stake their evil claims, battle each other, devour each other, haul every earthly horror. But thirty feet below sea level, their power ceases, their influence fades, their domination vanishes! Ah,

sir, live! Live in the heart of the seas! Here alone do I find independence! Here I recognize no superiors! Here I'm free! Jules Verne, Twenty Thousand Leagues Under the Seas, 1870

SUBTERRANEAN WORLDS (the cathonic realm) are found globally in myth and religion. Subterranean literature, emerging in the 19th century, drew on these roots and emerging scientific ideas too, such Scotsman James Hutton's 1785 theory of Deep Time. Notable works include *Journey to the Centre of the Earth* (Faddei Bulgarin in 1825, and Jules Verne in 1864) and Lewis Carroll's 1865 *Alice's Adventures Underground* (later changed to *in Wonderland*). It is perhaps unsurprising therefore to find H. G. Wells once again toying with such things, here evolutionary throwbacks in hellishly warm subterranean caverns in *The Time Machine*:

> I came to a large open space, and striking another match, saw that I had entered a vast arched cavern, which stretched into utter darkness beyond the range of my light. The view I had of it was as much as one could see in the burning of a match… Great shapes like big machines rose out of the dimness, and cast grotesque black shadows, in which dim spectral Morlocks sheltered from the glare. The place, by the bye, was very stuffy and oppressive, and the faint halitus of freshly-shed blood was in the air. H. G. Wells, The Time Machine, 1899

While the terrible Morlocks live underground, the beautiful (but weak) Eloi frolic above the surface, the division of peoples above and below the ground laying the foundation for hundreds of later literary reworkings. H. P. Lovecraft's 1940 novel *The Mound*, for example, is a typically weird tale which depicts a gateway to K'n-yan, a subterranean civilization inhabited in part by the reanimated dead.

Settlements
farm, village, town, city

Humans live in a variety of ways. Some subsist on their own in the middle of nowhere, others cluster in dense conurbations. Settlement types impact the mood, character and narrative tone of a literary work.

CITIES are many and varied. Joyce Carol Oates once asked: *If the City is a text, how shall we read it?* Virginia Woolf was fascinated by their depiction:

> *Domes swell; church spires, white with age, mingle with the tapering, pencil-shaped chimneys of factories. One hears the roar and the resonance of London itself. Here at last, we have landed at that thick and formidable circle of ancient stone, where so many drums have beaten and heads have fallen, the Tower of London itself. This is the know, the clue, the hub of all those scattered miles of skeleton desolation and ant-like activity. Here growls and grumbles that rough city song that has called the ships from the sea and brought them to lie captive beneath its warehouses.* Virginia Woolf, The London Scene Essays, 1931-2

With vivid sensory description, the place *roars, growls and grumbles*, Woolf presents London as she sees it, while evoking its ancient past. Cities are:

> *... difficult to capture in a traditional realist novel, and why they're the perfect grist for modernist experimentation: the city resists being seen as pure architecture or pure activity. We mistake the city if we take it for mere setting or plot. The city is character; it breathes its own life, speaks in its own tongue, moves to its own rhythms.*
>
> Tyler Malone Lapham's Quarterly, , 2018

SUBURBIA has come to be synonymous with the uncanny. Consider the brightly colored houses of *Edward Scissorhands* or the disturbingly perfect abodes of the *Stepford Wives*. These settings have come to symbolize a middle class utopia-turned-dystopia, where simmering tensions in suffocating settings lead to resentment, affairs and violence. 'Perfect' family units mask a strangled individualism:

> *It's as if everybody'd made this tacit agreement to live in a state of total self-deception. The hell with reality! Let's have a whole bunch of cute little winding roads and cute little houses painted white and pink and baby blue; let's all be good consumers and have a lot of Togetherness.* Richard Yates, Revolutionary Road, 1961

TOWNS come in many shapes and forms—provincial, sleepy, dirty, old, vibrant, cosy, soulless, and so on. Small towns may be stifling, unambitious or even menacing (*see page 11*), or they might provide just the right amount of 'stage' without the intensity and complexity of city life. In the opening pages to his 1966 true crime nonfiction novel *In Cold Blood* Truman Capote presents Halcomb, Kansas, with cinematic granularity:

> *After rain, or when snowfalls thaw, the streets, unnamed, unshaded, unpaved, turn from the thickest dust into the direst mud. At one end of the town stands a stark old stucco structure, the roof of which supports an electric sign—DANCE—but the dancing has ceased and the advertisement has been dark for several years.*

This is vivid and realistic yet also plays perfectly on our imagination and shared cultural memory. You're *there* but don't want to stay too long.

VILLAGES and farming and fishing communities are often tight-knit groups, operating outside of the norms, values or even laws of mainstream society. They can be an oppressive petri dish, a perfect setting for a closed cast murder mystery, or an idyllic refuge from urban dysfunction:

> *And Raveloe was a village where many of the old echoes lingered, undrowned by new voices. Not that it was one of those barren parishes lying on the outskirts of civilization — inhabited by meagre sheep and thinly-scattered shepherds: on the contrary, it lay in the rich central plain of what we are pleased to call Merry England.* George Eliot, Silas Marner, 1861

HOUSES & ROOMS
mansion, house, cottage, flat, room

Houses, in fiction (and in life), very often represent their inhabitants. Many houses are so significant to the narrative that they become eponymous – think novels like *Wuthering Heights, Mansfield Park, Howard's End,* and films and television series such as *Downton Abbey, Gosford Park* and *Saltburn.* Here is Henry James on the **ENGLISH COUNTRY HOUSE**:

> Of all the great things that the English have invented and made part of the credit of the national character, the most perfect, the most characteristic, the only one they have mastered completely in all its details, so that it becomes a compendious illustration of their social genius and their manners, is the well-appointed, well-administered, well-filled country house.

The country house continues to be a popular setting. The 'upstairs, downstairs' existence forces members of opposing classes to live cheek by jowl, creating tensions and intrigues, affairs, secrets and jealousies, creating a pressure cooker for human emotion. A country house contains a limited cast of characters living in relative isolation, allowing a writer to control the periphery of the story world setting . Agatha Christie uses this to her advantage, in her first detective novel *The Mysterious Affair at Styles.*

Houses are regularly personified: *The vast facade of the house stared coldly over its mounting lawns* writes Elizabeth Bowen in *The Last September (1929),* indeed **TOWN HOUSES** too can have discernable character:

> An uninhabited house of two storeys stood at the blind end, detached from its neighbours in a square ground. The other houses of the street, conscious of decent lives within them, gazed at one another with brown imperturbable faces.

James Joyce, Araby, 1914

ROOMS can develop characterisation, hold great symbolism and hide secrets, e.g. Rochester's **ATTIC** in *Jane Eyre*. Bedrooms are the heart of the hidden self—where a character is at their most vulnerable, where they dress, where they sleep and dream, where they are intimate. In the first Inspector Morse novel, the victim's bedroom outlines her character and offers clues:

> *Several items of underwear draped the table and chair which, with a whitewood wardrobe, substantively comprised the only other furniture. Morse gingerly picked up a flimsy black bra lying on the chair...A pile of women's magazines was awkwardly stacked on the window-sill, and Morse cursorily flicked his way through make-up hints, personal problems and horoscopes...He opened the wardrobe door and with perceptibly deeper interest examined the array of skirts, blouses, slacks and dresses. Clean and untidy. Mounds of shoes, ultramodern, wedged, ugly: she wasn't short of money.* Colin Dexter, The Last Train to Woodstock, 1975

QUESTIONS TO CONSIDER WHEN CRAFTING A HOME SETTING

1. A character should feel at home in their personal space, but what if they don't. Why could this be?
2. How many people live here? And pets, plants, pests, poltergeists?
3. Does the building stand out in the neighborhood, and why? Consider Toni Morrison's example from Beloved: 'a driver whipped his horse into the gallop local people felt necessary when they passed 124'.
4. Is this home ordered and tidy, or unkempt and falling apart? Neatness does not always spell a happy mind. In Roald Dahl's short story The Landlady extreme neatness belies a dark secret.
5. How is this home furnished? Are there antiques, paintings and collectibles, or is it gleaming with newness?
6. What is the center of the home? Where do the characters spend their time? Is it the kitchen, a cosy snug sofa, the bedroom?
7. Are there idiosyncrasies? An old servants' bell, a creaking floorboard, a hidden basement, a changeable smell, a jammed window?
8. Is this a home which receives guests regularly or is it a haven of isolation? What tells us this?
9. Is this house warm or cold (literally and metaphorically)?

INSTITUTIONS
schools, hospitals, prisons, temples, offices

HOSPITALS are places of life, death, hope, despair, science and emotion. As *principal setting* their revolving doors suit TV dramas, with bedsides, consultation rooms and operating theatres all pulsating with human drama:

> *Every observer I later talked to remembers this moment in Theater 3, when the air stood still, when the loud clock across from the table froze and a long, silent pause followed.* Abraham Verghese, *Cutting for stone*, 2009

Prose writers are drawn more towards 'the insane'. Samuel Pepys' diary from 19 February 1669 notes a tourist trade around the infamous Bedlam Hospital in London: *the young people went to see Bedlam, and at night home to them and to supper, and pretty merry.* For ASYLUMS, and their like, are 'islands of the mind' where residents are 'disturbed' as much by their own troubles (real or perceived) as the alien environment in which they find themselves:

> *I hear noise at the ward door, off up the hall out of my sight. That ward door starts opening at eight and opens and closes a thousand times a day, kashash, click. Every morning we sit lined up on each side of the day room, mixing jigsaw puzzles after breakfast, listen for a key to hit the lock, and wait to see what's coming in. There's not a whole lot else to do.* Ken Kesey, *One Flew Over the Cuckoo's Nest*, 1962

Susannah Kaysen's 1993 *Girl, Interrupted*, is also set in a psychiatric hospital:

> *...a parallel universe. There are so many of them: worlds of the insane, the criminal, the crippled, the dying, perhaps of the dead as well. These worlds exist alongside this world and resemble it, but are not in it.* Susannah Kaysen, *Girl Interrupted*, 1993

RELIGIOUS INSTITUTIONS are excellent settings for intrigue. Umberto Eco's *The Name of the Rose* and Ellis Peters' *Cadfael* both use religious or spiritual isolation—with a set number of confined characters—in much the same way Agatha Christie uses the English Country house for a murder mystery. Sylvia Townsend Warner's 1948 novel *The Corner that Held Them*, set in a struggling medieval nunnery, examines spirituality and communal living in general:

> But the prioress continued to express pleasure in Dame Alice's common sense, candour, and lack of imagination, so Dame Alice continued to manifest common sense and lack of imagination. Sylvia Townsend Warner, The Corner that Held Them, 1948

PRISON settings often feature some underlying currents of dark humor alongside descriptions of physical deprivation and brutality:

> ...in a sheltered spot to keep the readings from being too low, the thermometer hung, caked over with ice. Shukhov gave a hopeful sidelong glance at the milk-white tube. If it went down to forty-two below zero they weren't supposed to be marched out to work. But today the thermometer wasn't pushing forty or anything like it.
> Alexander Solzhenitsyn, One Day in the Life of Ivan Denisovich, 1962

Solzhenitsyn's gulag is a 'camp', designed to de-humanise its inhabitants, complete with menacing guard towers, barbed wired, and search lights.

Tom Brown's first view of his new study room at a 19th century British public SCHOOL can hardly compare to a Russian penal colony, but children are locked in schools every day; there are subtle parallels with a prison life:

> It wasn't very large, certainly, being about six feet long by four broad. It couldn't be called light, as there were bars and a grating to the window; which little precautions were necessary in the studies on the ground-floor looking out into the close, to prevent the exit of small boys after locking up, and the entrance of contraband articles.
> Thomas Hughes, Tom Brown's School Days, 1857

Like all of the above, OFFICE settings brim with monotony, routine, hierarchy, power dynamics, and dreams of ambition and escape.

Liminal Places
on the edge, in between, not at all

LIMINAL SPACES make for compelling literary settings. They are often boundary or transition, like a gateway, crossroads or river, the edge of a wood, a derelict house or graveyard, a break in a battle, dawn, twilight.

In Michael Ondaatje's 1992 *The English Patient* (a novel where atmosphere is character) the bombed out *Villa San Girolamo, built to protect inhabitants from the flesh of the devil*, plays host to vivid flashbacks and character epithanies. War is giving way to peace and the protagonist lays dying, the old villa echoing a profound sense of suspension between two worlds:

> *There seemed little demarcation between house and landscape, between damaged building and the burned and shelled remnants of the earth. To Hana the wild gardens were like further rooms. She worked along the edges of them aware always of unexploded mines.* Michael Ondaatje, *The English Patient*, 1992

Coastlines and shores have long been viewed as sacred or transitional zones, twixt earth and water. Andrew Hurley's 2014 novel *The Loney* plays on this in a modern setting—a desolate stretch of coast in northwest England:

> *Dull and featureless it may have looked, but the Loney was a dangerous place. A wild and useless length of English coastline. A dead mouth of a bay that filled and emptied twice a day and made Coldbarrow—a desolate spit of land a mile off the coast—into an island. The tides could come in quicker than a horse could run and every year a few people drowned.* Andrew Hurley, *The Loney*, 2014

Thomas Mann uses shoreline as metaphor to mark beginning and end:

> *… he looked over his shoulder towards the shore. The watcher sat there, as he had sat once before when for the first time these twilight-grey eyes had turned at the doorway and met his own.* Thomas Mann, *Death in Venice*, 1912

Forests, wrote critic Anne Barton, *are places of transformation, where the boundary between human life and that of animals, plants or trees are likely to become confused, or even obliterated.* Shakespeare sets *A Midsummer's Night Dream* in a magical woodland. Max's bedroom turns into a forest in Maurice Sendak's 1963 classic *Where the Wild Things Are*. Robert Frost's 1922 poem *Stopping by the Woods on a Snowy Evening* captures something of their dark magic:

> *The woods are lovely, dark and deep, / But I have promises to keep,*
> *And miles to go before I sleep, / And miles to go before I sleep.*

Some narratives take liminality to the extreme and **DENY SETTING** altogether, keeping things vague, timeless and placeless, so we project our own images into the narrative. Shirley Jackson's 1948 short story *The Lottery* takes place on June 27th, but resolutely resists further dating. We find ourselves in a seemingly bucolic rural idyll, people have running water, neat homes, handmade artifacts. However, the tone is a little disturbing. Are we in a post apocalyptic society or an early twentieth century village?

> *Soon the men began to gather, surveying their own children, speaking of planting and rain, tractors and taxes. They stood together, away from the pile of stones in the corner, and their jokes were quiet and they smiled rather than laughed. The women, wearing faded house dresses and sweaters, came shortly after their menfolk. They greeted one another and exchanged bits of gossip as they went to join their husbands.*

In Samuel Beckett's 1952 play *Waiting for Godot* we know we are by a barren tree on an empty country road, but Beckett avoids date and time indicators to give the sense that our characters wait in perpetuity, and will continue to do so long after the play finishes.

ON THE ROAD
setting as metaphor

Roads, ancient and modern, and the journeys taken upon them, bear witness to adventure, self discovery, and change. The road is a catalyst for drama. In the Bible, Saul has his epiphany en route to Damascus:

> *As he came near the city, suddenly a light shone around him from heaven. Then he fell to the ground, and heard a voice saying to him ...*

In Jack Kerouac's 1957 *On the Road* the road is a way of being: *Nothing behind me, everything ahead of me, as is ever so on the road.* In *The Wizard of Oz* we find a more tangible yellow brick version where characters overcome hardship in a classic telling of **THE HERO'S AND HEROINE'S JOURNEY** (see sister books *Plot* and *Character*)—the road as metaphor for life journey.

Narratives in which "the journey" is forefront can be viewed as using setting as backdrop, or as pastiche, despite the fact that the journey still takes place within and around a moving person, car, train, boat or plane, and also within some larger setting, e.g. a desert, as here:

> *We were somewhere around Barstow on the edge of the desert when the drugs began to take hold. I remember saying something like "I feel a bit lightheaded; maybe you should drive...." And suddenly there was a terrible roar all around us and the sky was full of what looked like huge bats, all swooping and screeching and diving around the car, which was going about a hundred miles an hour with the top down to Las Vegas.* Hunter S. Thompson, Fear and Loathing in Las Vegas, 1971

Junctions in the road symbolize decision-making. Robert Frost's 1915 poem *The Road Not Taken* shapes the profundity of the metaphor:

> *Two roads diverged in a yellow wood, / And sorry I could not travel both*
> *And be one traveler, long I stood / And looked down one as far as I could*
> *To where it bent in the undergrowth*

The poem is most famous for its end lines *Two roads diverged in a wood, and I / took the one less traveled by / And that has made all the difference*, often taken to mean that one should plough one's own furrow in life, not feel obliged to follow the herd; although, in the end, of course, one never knows.

A road can also represent conformity and safety. Allegorically, Little Red Riding Hood is a warning not to stray from the woodland path. Feminist writers, such as Angela Carter, have opposed this diktat as a symbol of the compliant female.

In Cormac McCarthy's dystopic 2006 novel *The Road*, the eponymous setting is a sign of safety and security for the two travelers—a symbol of the now collapsed past. As with the Red Riding Hood story, straying from it can mean straying from safety and from human decency as survivors turn on one another. In this story though, the road itself can hold dangers as the man and boy carry 'the light' of their hope and decency to the end of their journey:

> *He got up and walked out to the road. The black shape of it running from dark to dark. Then the distant low rumble. Not thunder. You could feel it under your feet. A sound without cognate and so without description. Something imponderable shifting out there in the dark. The earth itself contracting with the cold. It did not come again. What time of year? What age the child? He walked out into the road and stood. The silence. The salitter drying from the earth. The mudstained shapes of flooded cities burned to the waterline. At a crossroads a ground set with dolmen stones where the spoken bones of oracles lay moldering. No sound but the wind.*

Cormac McCarthy. The Road, 2006

Altered Settings
is there any tea on this spaceship?

Embedding unreal events and characters within a recognizable setting (p.22) is a reliable technique for suspending disbelief. Mary Shelley's *Frankenstein* opens in frozen tundra but also takes us to the German city of Ingolstadt (where the creature is created), Geneva (where Victor Frankenstein grew up), the Orkney Islands, and the Irish shore. These real places frame Shelley's Gothic tale, making it more plausible and creating a sense of uncanniness, what Freud (building on the work of Ernst Jentsch) calls the UNHEIMLICH, a world both familiar and unfamiliar at the same time:

> *It was on a dreary night of November that I beheld the accomplishment of my toils. With an anxiety that almost amounted to agony, I collected the instruments of life around me, that I might infuse a spark of being into the lifeless thing that lay at my feet. It was already one in the morning; the rain pattered dismally against the panes, and my candle was nearly burnt out, when, by the glimmer of the half-extinguished light, I saw the dull yellow eye of the creature open; it breathed hard, and a convulsive motion agitated its limbs.* Mary Shelley, Frankenstein, 1818

Recognisable settings can also be manipulated to create new worlds which are themselves uncanny, places we know and yet don't know.

In Philip Pullman's *His Dark Materials* trilogy we encounter a version of Oxford—a symbolic location synonymous with scholarship and social hierarchy—inhabited by humans and their animal daemons. There are zeppelins instead of cars, and the clothing is a version of Edwardian English costume. Many Oxford colleges, The Ashmolean Museum, the Botanical Gardens and university Parks, landmarks of the real city, feature in the parallel geography. There is a quiet joy for the reader in both recognizing place and being immersed in a strange new world.

> And now that Lyra had the taste for exploring it, she abandoned her usual haunt, the irregular alps of the College roofs, and plunged with Roger into this netherworld. ... One day she and Roger made their way into the crypt below the oratory. This was where generations of Masters had been buried, each in his lead-lined oak coffin in niches along the stone walls ... On each coffin, Lyra was interested to see, a brass plaque bore a picture of a different being: this one a basilisk, this a serpent, this a monkey. She realized that they were images of the dead men's dæmons. As people became adult, their dæmons lost the power to change and assumed one shape, keeping it permanently. Philip Pulman, The Golden Compass, 1995

In *Jonathan Strange and Mr Norrell*, Susannah Clarke lightly injects the other-worldly use of magic and the presence of the ethereal Raven King into the wholly recognisable world of nineteenth century England.

> SOME YEARS AGO there was in the city of York a society of magicians. They met upon the third Wednesday of every month and read each other long, dull papers upon the history of English magic. Susannah Clarke, Jonathan Strange and Mr Norrell, 2004

In her *Harry Potter* books J. K. Rowling draws on London locations, such as King's Cross Station, to smooth the transition to her fantasy world. Film adaptions make potent use of such settings. Here Harry gets advice on how to access 'platform nine and three-quarters':

> "... walk straight at the barrier between platforms nine and ten. Don't stop and don't be scared you'll crash into it, that's very important. Best do it at a bit of a run if you're nervous. Go on, go now before Ron."
>
> Harry Potter and the Philosopher's Stone, 1997

Fantasy Settings
hobbits, elves, vulcans & yoda

In a fantasy setting anything goes. The author is limited only by their imagination and their ability to communicate and ground their vision for their reader. Disappearing cats, supernatural powers, magical objects, dragons, dwarves, fairies, fauns, giants and talking lions are all fair game:

> 'Here is Nimrodel!' said Legolas. 'Of this stream the Silvan Elves made many songs long ago, and still we sing them in the North, remembering the rainbow on its falls, and the golden flowers that floated in its foam. All is dark now and the Bridge of Nimrodel is broken down. I will bathe my feet, for it is said that the water is healing to the weary.' He went forward and climbed down the deep cloven bank and stepped into the stream. J. R. R. Tolkien, The Lord of the Rings, 1954

While some fantasy settings encompass a novel's whole world (*as above*, or e.g. *The Game of Thrones*), others exist as **PARALLEL WORLDS**, accessed from our own world via a **PORTAL**: e.g. a wardrobe (*Narnia*), a railway station (*Harry Potter*), a rabbit hole (*Alice in Wonderland*), a special path (*'second star on the right and then straight on 'til morning'*) or an incantation or magical implement (*The Subtle Knife*). Such portals can be a metaphor for the transition between childhood and adulthood, and a lament that this portal can become a hard border far too soon. Here, Puddlegum, a marshwiggle in C. S. Lewis' *The Silver Chair*, defends such fantasies in defiance of the Green Witch:

> Suppose we have only dreamed, or made up, all those things — trees and grass and sun and moon and stars and Aslan himself. Suppose we have. Then all I can say is that, in that case, the made-up things seem a good deal more important than the real ones. Suppose this black pit of a kingdom of yours is the only world. Well, it strikes me as a pretty poor one. And that's a funny thing, when you come to think of it. We're just babies making up a game, if you're right. But four babies playing a game can make

a play-world which licks your real world hollow. That's why I'm going to stand by the play-world. I'm on Aslan's side even if there isn't any Aslan to lead it. I'm going to live as like a Narnian as I can even if there isn't any Narnia. C. S. Lewis, The Silver Chair, 1953

We do not always have to transition into other worlds, particularly if the message is not as allegorical as these examples from children's fiction. Mervyn Peake's *Gormenghast* plunges us immediately into a gigantic castle:

> Gormenghast....*the shadows of time-eaten buttresses, of broken and lofty turrets, and, most enormous of all, the shadow of the Tower of Flints. This tower patched unevenly with black ivy, arose like a mutilated finger from among the fists of knuckled masonry and pointed blasphemously at heaven.* Mervyn Peake, Gormenghast, 1950

The world contained within the castle walls is at once recognizable and utterly bizarre, by releasing himself from the fetters of reality Peake can create characters and plot elements simply not possible in our world.

At the heart of fantasy writing is the art of **WORLDBUILDING**. Authors like Jonathan Swift and J.R.R. Tolkien created maps, peoples, genealogies, religions and entire languages to flesh out their settings:

> *To make a Secondary World inside which the green sun will be credible, commanding Secondary Belief, will probably require labour and thought, and will certainly demand a special skill, a kind of elvish craft. Few attempt such difficult tasks. But when they are attempted and in any degree accomplished then we have a rare achievement of Art: indeed narrative art, storymaking in its primary and most potent mode.* On Fairy Stories, J.R.R.Tolkien, 1939

The following pages contain some questions and exercises for any authors who might be starting to building their own worlds and settings.

EXERCISES
for developing setting

QUESTIONS FOR WORLD BUILDING

Important: Ensure you know your world intimately, so that it is CONSISTENT. If a setting has a poisonous atmosphere don't allow someone to wander freely about without breathing apparatus. Know it, and know it well. The rule of thumb is that you gradually release between 5-10% of all that you know about your world. A lecture at the beginning detailing everything is clumsy and off-putting, sprinkling information essential to the plot throughout is far more effective.

Rules and laws - What are the rules of this society? What counts as a crime and who defines this? Are there unwritten rules - social practices and expectations? Taboos and sins? What typifies a good citizen here? What about the laws of physics - is gravity the same? How does time work here?

Environment - Is this a green world or a barren one? Desert, rural, agricultural, urban or industrial? Are the people at one with their environment or struggling against it? What is the weather like? Are there recognizable seasons?

Culture - What do people in this setting believe in? What are their religious practices , if they have them? What do they value? Is there art, music, literature?

Language - What is the main tongue in this world? There will always be dialects based on geography and social group - what are the features of these dialects and who speaks them? Are there prejudices based around these? Who 'controls' language and how has it developed here?

History - How has this world developed? Is there a history of conflict? Are they in a golden age or following the collapse of a great society? Are there long-running rivalries and alliances?

Races and Subcultures - A great pitfall for worldbuilders lies in creating the sense that all in a world are the same, unless you are trying to create a disturbing world full of identical beings remember that a truly convincing world is one full of contrast and variation. What are the factions in society? Are there religious/racial/gender/age groups?

Geography - As above, presumably your world will not be the same wherever one travels. Are there particular 'zones'? What is the topography like? Do we have mountains, lakes, seas and shores? Are there abandoned or no-go areas? If there are towns and cities, how are they planned? Thomas More's *Utopia* is particularly strong in this regard.

- **Resources** - What do the inhabitants of this city need and how do they get it? Do they need food, water, and fuel as humans do? Is there a tension which lies in the acquisition of resources?

- **Flora and Fauna** - Do these exist? If so, what are they like and how do characters interact with them? Have they developed over time or are there ancient beasts and plants? Are these friend or foe to our characters?

- **Place names** - In our sister book, *Character*, we discussed how character names can tell us a lot. The same might be true of place. We often name places with sounds which correspond to their physical characteristics. A stony outcrop might contain lots of fricative 'f' and 'v' sounds, or some guttural 'g's, Tolkien's Sauron rules over the doom-laden land or Mordor and his characters travel through the devastated deadly Mines of Moria. Homer tells of a wonderful afterlife land called Elysium.

EXERCISES IN SETTING

- **Perspective** - Think of a particular memory that you have. Using the examples of different perspectives on page 15 as inspiration describe the setting of that memory from three different angles:
  - From the ground - a conventional description
  - From a bird's eye view
  - From an unusual angle which offers a different perspective, through a window; through the bottom of a pint glass; from a literal fly on the wall?

- **Room Recall** - Think of a room which you have occupied recently, not one that you know well but one as unfamiliar to you as a setting would be to your reader. Think about what you can remember of that room.
  - How did it feel?
  - What elements of the room contributed to that?
  - Now describe the room
  Remember that you are looking for a broad picture with a few micro-details to capture the essence, not a witness statement. Describe the room:

- **Outside Settings** - Think of the last place you were outside in the open air.
  - List the essential elements of light and sensation?
  - Write an impressionist description of it (see p.15)
  - Write a realist description of the same place

- **Static setting** - Think about somewhere you have revisited throughout your life, and the different occasions you were there.
  - Has it changed, have you changed?
  - Note down the most significant occasions
  - Describe each briefly.

- **Character and Setting** - Think of someone you know but whose house you have never seen before. This might be an acquaintance, a celebrity, a personal hero, etc. Based on what you know of their character, what do you think

their home will look like from the outside?
- Choose one room in the house, and imagine it is a sunny day.
- 'Dress' it (describe it) to fit their personality.
- Describe the same room at night.

Observation - Sit quietly somewhere that you know very well, this can be indoors or outside.
- Look at it closely.
- Identify three things about it you've never noticed before.
- Identify three things which change while you sit there.

Time - Choose a well known location which has some history.
- Describe it as a setting today
- Describe it 100 years ago
- Describe it 250 years ago
- Describe it in 100 years time
Think about how not only what you would see is different but what your sensory experiences would be, how people would talk and behave.

The Senses - Practice writing without visuals. Using the senses other than sight is a great way of showing instead of telling and is an important part of your setting arsenal.
- Imagine walking down a street you know only using sound
- Imagine walking along the same street only using smell
- Describe the street only using sound and smell
  - Describe the street using only touch

Change the Mood - Think of somewhere which has a lot of emotional significance to you. Notice the mood this place evokes in you.
- Write a description of it which evokes this mood
- Now describe it to evoke the opposite mood

Change the Setting - Pick an important scene from your work. Now:
- Imagine it in the setting you originally envisaged
- Describe the same scene in another setting, nearby
- Now describe it another country with a different climate

Change the Weather - Think of a setting you associate with a particular season, e.g. a beach you know well because you visit it in the summer.
- Describe it as you think of it
- Describe it throughout each of the different seasons, consider how it changes
- Choose one season and toy with it, subverting the weather. A dismally rainy summer day, bright sunshine in December, for example.

Make a Map - Imagine the world of your story and the places in it.
- On a large sheet of paper, draw a map of that world
- At the key locations draw sketches of the places, or, if you are no artist, write key descriptive words
- Add more and more detail until you fill the sheet